GRANITE

Tracy Vonder Brink

NorwoodHouse Press

Cataloging-in-Publication Data

Names: Vonder Brink, Tracy.
Title: Granite / Tracy Vonder Brink.
Description: Buffalo, NY : Norwood House Press, 2027. | Series: Earth's rocks | Includes glossary and index.
Identifiers: ISBN 9781978580053 (pbk.) | ISBN 9781978580060 (library bound) | ISBN 9781978580077 (ebook)
Subjects: LCSH: Igneous rocks--Juvenile literature. | Magmatism--Juvenile literature.
Classification: LCC QE461.V66 2027 | DDC 552.1--dc23

Published in 2027 by
Norwood House Press
2544 Clinton Street
Buffalo, NY 14224

Designer: Rhea Magaro
Editor: Kim Thompson

Photo credits: Cover, p. 1 Dancestrokes/Shutterstock.com; p. 3 LesPalenik/Shutterstock.com; p. 4 Kavic.C/Shutterstock.com; p. 5 Marco Ritzki/Shutterstock.com; p. 6 vilax/Shutterstock.com; p. 8 BlueRingMedia/Shutterstock.com; p. 9 papa papong/Shutterstock.com; p. 10 JStagg_Photography/Shutterstock.com; p. 11 LUC KOHNEN/Shutterstock.com; p. 12 kevin brine/Shutterstock.com; p. 13 Taras Kushnir/Shutterstock.com; p. 14 Felix Lipov/Shutterstock.com; p. 15 Isogood_patrick/Shutterstock.com; p. 16 CK Foto/Shutterstock.com; p. 17 Vladislav T. Jirousek/Shutterstock.com; p. 18 Joseph GTK/Shutterstock.com; p. 19 Marcel Hamonic/Shutterstock.com; p. 21 Artazum/Shutterstock.com;

Printed in the United States of America

TABLE OF CONTENTS

What Is Granite? 4

How Does Granite Form? 8

Where Is Granite Found? 14

How Is Granite Used? 18

Glossary 22

Thinking Questions 23

Index 24

About the Author 24

WHAT IS GRANITE?

Rocks make up many things in the world, from tall mountains to the deep seafloor. All rocks are made of **minerals**. They are put into three main groups based on how they form.

Types of Rock

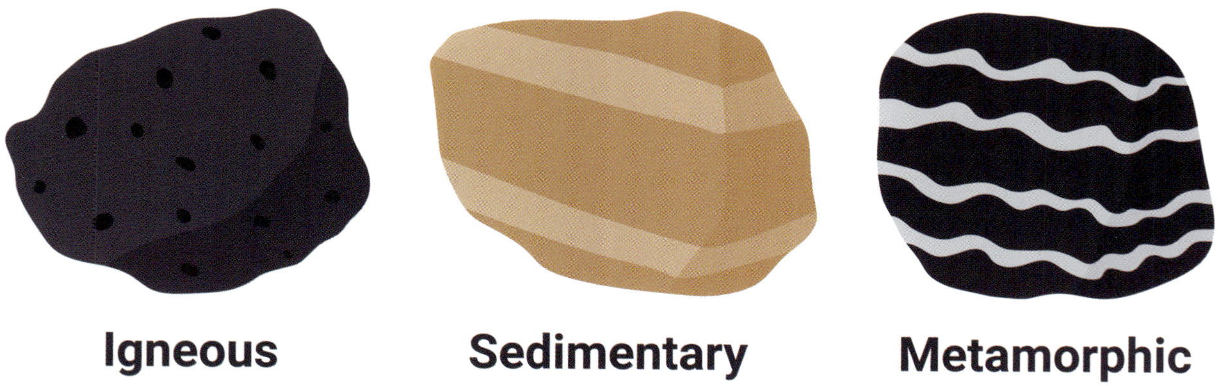

Igneous means "fire." Igneous rocks form from **magma** or lava. Granite is an igneous rock.

Granite has large mineral **crystals** that can be seen without a magnifying glass. Granite comes in many colors. It may be black, gray, green, or look like salt and pepper. Granite can even be pink.

HOW DOES GRANITE FORM?

Like all rocks, granite forms during Earth's rock cycle.

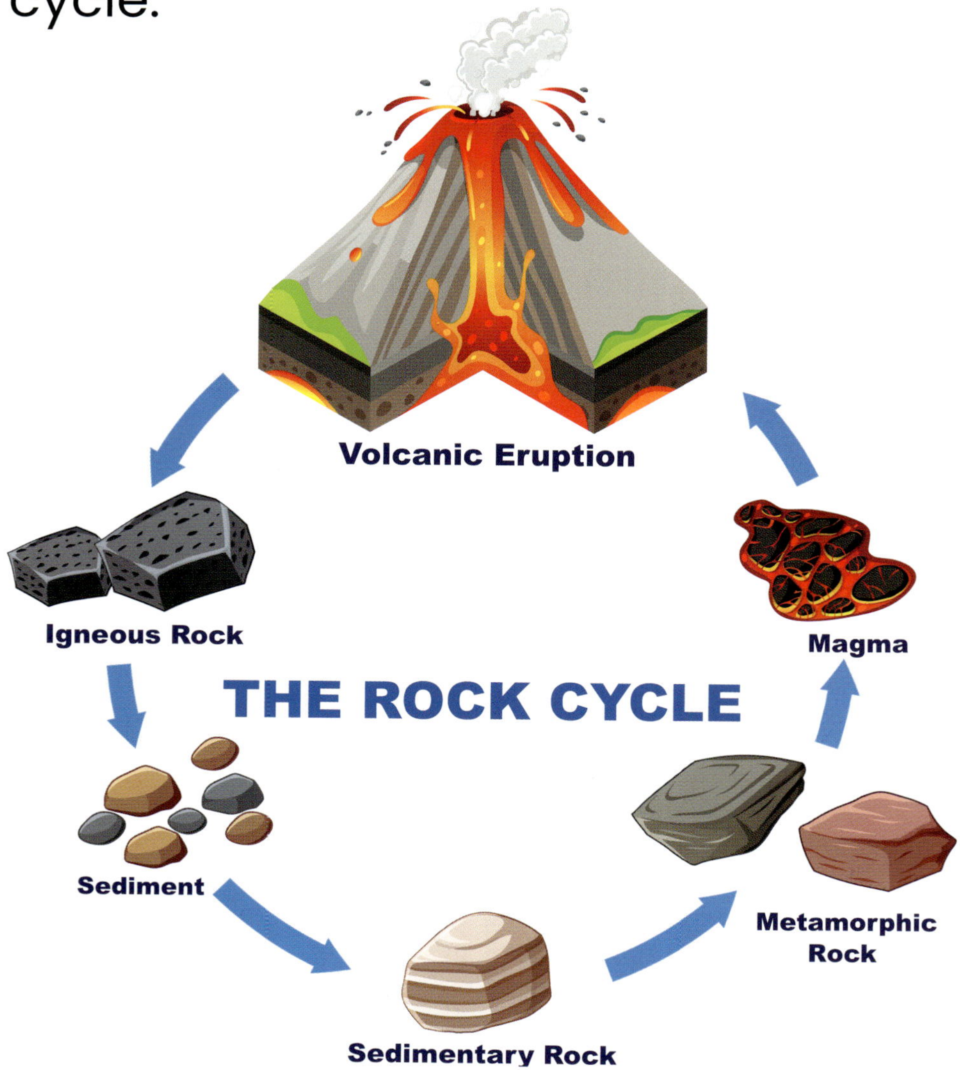

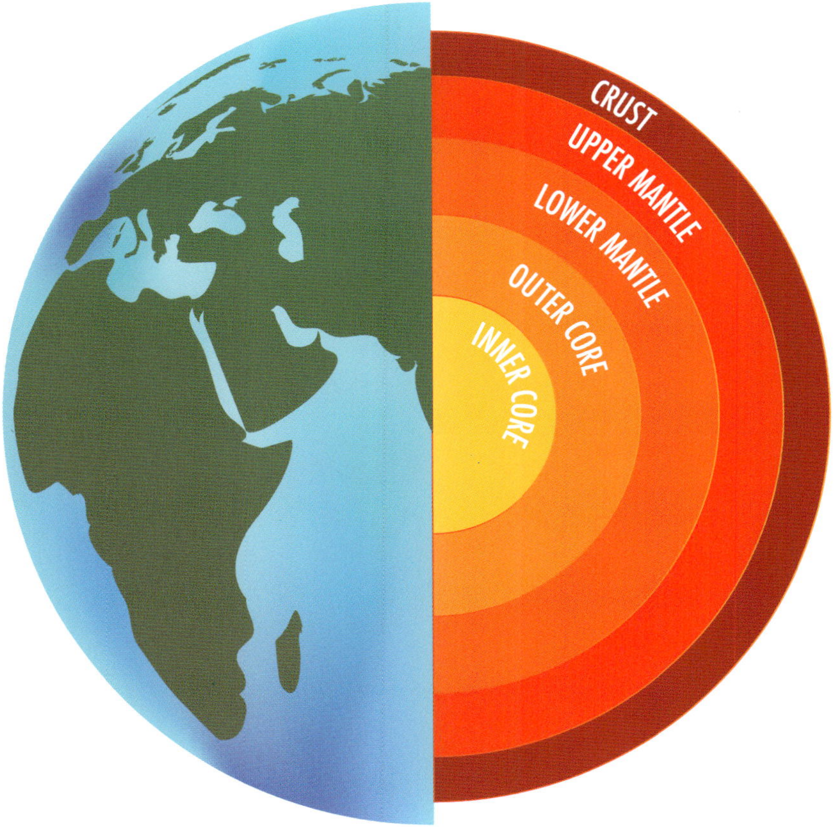

Part of the rock cycle takes place in Earth's mantle, deep inside the planet. Earth has layers. The crust is on top. The mantle lies below. It's so hot in the mantle that rock melts into magma.

Magma rises because it's less **dense** than the rock above it. Some magma stops before it reaches Earth's surface.

Magma that gets trapped underground cools over millions of years. It hardens into rock. Some becomes granite.

As they cool, minerals inside the magma form crystals. As long as the magma stays hot, the crystals keep growing. They stop growing when the magma becomes rock.

Granite has large crystals because it cools slowly, giving crystals more time to grow.

WHERE IS GRANITE FOUND?

Granite is found in mountains around the world. As these mountains formed, **uplift** made granite rise from below Earth's surface.

Granite makes up most of the Sierra Nevada Mountain Range in the United States.

El Capitan is one of its famous granite peaks. It stands 7,569 feet (2,307 meters) tall.

Wind, rain, and ice can wear away softer rock layers that cover granite. After millions of years, only the granite is left.

Karlu Karlu, also known as Devils Marbles, is in Australia. It formed as other rocks **eroded**, leaving only granite **boulders** behind.

HOW IS GRANITE USED?

Granite is very hard. It doesn't break easily. That's why people have built with it for thousands of years. Ancient Egyptians used granite to build pyramids.

Granite is also used for statues and **monuments**. Mount Rushmore in the U.S. was carved from a granite mountain.

Granite is crushed and used to make roads. Granite may even be in your kitchen. Cut, polished granite is often used for countertops.

Granite is all around you. It is strong, useful, and beautiful.

GLOSSARY

boulders (BOHL-durz): large, rounded rocks

crystals (KRIS-tuhls): substances that form patterns of many flat surfaces as they become solids; salt and quartz are examples of crystals

dense (dens): heavier than many things of a similar size

eroded (i-ROH-did): worn away gradually by water and wind

magma (MAG-muh): melted rock below Earth's surface that becomes lava when it flows out of volcanoes

minerals (MIN-ur-uhlz): solids that form naturally in Earth and that do not come from an animal or plant; granite contains minerals such as quartz and feldspar

monuments (MAHN-yuh-muhnts): statues, buildings, or other structures built to remind people of important people and events

uplift (UHP-lift): the raising of Earth's surface in response to natural causes

THINKING QUESTIONS

1. How are rocks put into groups?
2. What does granite look like?
3. Why does magma rise?
4. Why does granite have large crystals?
5. Describe some of the ways people use granite.

INDEX

colors 7

countertops 20

crystals 7, 12, 13

erosion 16, 17

igneous 4, 5, 8

magma 5, 8–12

minerals 4, 7, 12

monuments 19

mountains 4, 14, 15, 19

rock cycle 8, 9

ABOUT THE AUTHOR

Tracy Vonder Brink is always curious about the world around her. She loves to make facts and true stories fun and has written many books for kids. Tracy lives near Cincinnati, Ohio, and enjoys reading, hiking, and playing with her two rescue dogs.